ALEXANDER HAMILTON

THE OUTSIDER

Jean Fritz

ALEXANDER HAMILTON

THE OUTSIDER

ILLUSTRATIONS BY

Ian Schoenherr

PUFFIN BOOKS
An Imprint of Penguin Group (USA) Inc.

ACKNOWLEDGMENTS

I acknowledge my indebtedness to the following:

Major Colin Williams, United States Military Academy at West Point,
for his critical reading of the manuscript;

Major Aram Donigian, United States Military Academy at West Point,
for finding Colin and for being one of my most loyal readers;

Ian Schoenherr, who shares my love of American history,
reflected in his fine illustrations and in his collection of historical prints;

and my longtime editor, Margaret Frith,
for her unfailing interest in the manuscript.

Puffin Books
Published by the Penguin Group
Penguin Young Readers Group, 345 Hudson Street, New York, New York 10014, U.S.A.
Penguin Group (Canada), 90 Eglinton Avenue East, Suite 700, Toronto, Ontario, Canada M4P 2Y3
(a division of Pearson Penguin Canada Inc.)
Penguin Books Ltd, 80 Strand, London WC2R 0RL, England
Penguin Ireland, 25 St Stephen's Green, Dublin 2, Ireland (a division of Penguin Books Ltd)
Penguin Group (Australia), 250 Camberwell Road, Camberwell, Victoria 3124, Australia
(a division of Pearson Australia Group Pty Ltd)
Penguin Books India Pvt Ltd, 11 Community Centre, Panchsheel Park, New Delhi - 110 017, India
Penguin Group (NZ), 67 Apollo Drive, Rosedale, Auckland 0632, New Zealand (a division of Pearson New Zealand Ltd.)
Penguin Books (South Africa) (Pty) Ltd, 24 Sturdee Avenue, Rosebank, Johannesburg 2196, South Africa

Registered Offices: Penguin Books Ltd, 80 Strand, London WC2R 0RL, England

First published in the United States of America by G. P. Putnam's Sons, a division of Penguin Young Readers Group, 2011
Published by Puffin Books, a division of Penguin Young Readers Group, 2012

13 15 17 19 20 18 16 14 12

Text copyright © Jean Fritz, 2011
Illustrations copyright © Ian Schoenherr, 2011
All rights reserved

THE LIBRARY OF CONGRESS HAS CATALOGED THE G. P. PUTNAM'S SONS EDITION AS FOLLOWS:
Fritz, Jean.
Alexander Hamilton : the outsider / Jean Fritz ; illustrations by Ian Schoenherr.
p.   cm.
1. Hamilton, Alexander, 1757–1804—Juvenile literature. 2. Statesmen—United States—Biography—Juvenile literature.
3. United States—History—Revolution, 1775–1783—Juvenile literature.
4. United States—Politics and government—1783–1809—Juvenile literature. I. Schoenherr, Ian, ill. II. Title.
ISBN 978-0-399-25546-5 (hc)
E302.6.H2F86 2011
973.4092—dc22 [B] 2010006008

Puffin Books ISBN 978-0-14-241986-1

Design by Ryan Thomann. Text set in Italian Old Style.

Printed in the United States of America

This book is dedicated to my daughter Andrea,
without whom the book could not have been written.

—J.F.

Preface

My family history includes Hamiltons in Colonial America; this has led some relatives to claim Alexander Hamilton as an ancestor. Whether or not there are blood ties, we are proud to acknowledge his place in American history.

The more I learned about Alexander Hamilton, the more impressed I became. He is a man of great contradictions, which show up in his feelings about war. I had to struggle with the many quirks and complexities in his character, but I came away from the work fully convinced of Hamilton's contributions to our country and his unwavering sense of justice. If I could have one wish for the present generation, it would be that they are motivated by the same sense of justice and equally insistent on defending it.

—J.F.
Sleepy Hollow, NY
2010

Beginnings

MARYLAND
A MAP of the
WEST-INDIES &
MEXICO or NEW SPAI
Also ye Trade Winds, and ye several
acts made by ye Galeons and Flota fro
Place to Place. By H.Moll Geograp
C. Charles
Bay of Chesapeak
Albemarle Sound
C. Hataras
C. Look out
C. Fear
Cartaret
Royal
Barmudas Is.
English
Variable Winds
ATLANTICK
OCEAN
BAHAMA
ISLANDS
Eleuthera
St. Salvador
Rum I.
Tropick of Can
Crooked I.
Maguana
Caicos B.
Heneago
C. Francis
C. Engano
French
HISPANIOLA
Spain
Saona
Mona
Boreque
St. Croix
Leeward Islands
Antego I.
Guardalupa I.
Marigalante I.
Dominica
Martenica I.
St. Lucia I.
Barbados
St. Vincent
Granada
Tabago
Trinidad
Antilles Isla
NORTH SEA
Caribbee I.
C. Vela
Lit. Antilles
Bonaire I.
Curassow I.
Aruba I.
New Granada
Truxillo
Caracos
New Andalusia
Mopox
St. Christoval
Tucuyo
TERRA FIRMA

CHAPTER ONE

Alexander Hamilton should have been born in his grandfather's fogbound castle on the west coast of Scotland, the same castle where his father, James, had been born, along with James's three older brothers. But as the fourth son, James would not stand a chance of inheriting even a share of the castle. That's the way it worked in Scotland.

Even so, young James was expected to help his brothers do the chores around the castle—exercise the horses, feed the dogs and look for lost sheep. Yet when his brothers called for

James to help them, where was he? Off. Away. Not around. He was playing—out of sight and out of hearing.

When James was nineteen, his brother John took him to Glasgow to become an apprentice in the linen industry. He had to agree to work there for four years. But the work didn't suit him, and when the time was up, he was ready to get as far away from Scotland as he could.

Off James went to St. Kitts in the West Indies, where there were supposed to be plenty of jobs on sugar plantations. James tried trading sugar but he wasn't very good at it. Instead of making money, he ended up owing money.

Then James met a local girl named Rachel. She had been married and divorced, and the terms of her divorce prevented her from ever marrying again. So Rachel and James lived together, calling themselves James and Rachel Hamilton. Eventually they had a son, called James, after his father.

They were living on Nevis by the time another son was born on January 11, 1755 (or 1757). They named him Alexander after his grandfather, and because it was a good Scottish name and sounded prosperous.

Alexander was a bright, curious, ambitious boy. He probably inherited his brains from Rachel, who was said to have been smart and clever.

Not until he was older would Alexander find that his

brains and his ambition would shape his life. At the moment, Alexander and his brother James were being tutored, not on a regular basis, but often enough so Alexander learned to read better than other boys his age. He didn't pronounce one letter at a time, as children were taught in school. He said the whole word at once. He especially liked doing sums. He loved the exactness and orderliness of numbers, marching them up and down in columns and watching them change in value as he added and subtracted.

He learned other things too. He may have been a superior student, but the community looked down on him and his family. Women who passed him and his brother on the street would whisper "obscene children." He knew this was because his father and mother were not married. For the same reason, boys would sometimes rub the forefinger of one hand against the forefinger of the other hand, a gesture that meant "shame!"

Alexander read as many books as he could—about kings, queens, war and how people might learn to live together. Later in life, when he became prominent in politics, Alexander Hamilton was often described as an "outsider" because of his West Indian background. Perhaps in one way or another he had been one since he was a boy. Not only because he didn't have a proper family, but also because he never felt as if he belonged in the West Indies.

Life was difficult, largely because there was little money. So when James Hamilton was offered a job on St. Croix, collecting money from a man in debt, the family went to St. Croix. Rachel's older sister, Ann Lytton, lived on the island with her husband, James. The Lyttons owned a grand house called the Grange. But they had money problems too. Not long after the Hamiltons arrived, they had to sell the Grange and move to Nevis.

A year later, when James Hamilton had collected the debt after a lawsuit, he left St. Croix alone, deserting his family forever. Sometimes Alexander and his father wrote to each other, but he never saw his father again.

But Rachel was resourceful. She and the boys moved to a building where Rachel opened a shop. Alexander, eleven years old and always good with numbers, began to keep her ledgers, order her goods and wait on her customers.

When an epidemic broke out in that part of the West Indies, both Rachel and Alexander came down with a fever. While he was sick, Alexander shared the one bed in their house with his mother while James continued to sleep on the floor. Rachel died after about three weeks.

On the day of his mother's funeral, still feeling ill and very aware of his poverty, Alexander had a glimpse of how wealthy his mother's family once must have been. Walking behind the mourners on the way to the grave, Alexander saw, as if for the first time, the Grange where the Lyttons had lived. It was a large, empty house with carved windows and carved doors. It must have been a very grand place.

Now that the funeral was over, the question was, what will happen to Alexander? Neither his father nor Rachel had made any provision for him or James. They were legally under the guardianship of their cousin Peter Lytton, but he paid little attention to them. And their half-brother (Rachel's son by her first marriage), Peter Lavien, arrived from South Carolina and claimed possession of Rachel's things, including the thirty-four books that Alexander loved. Fortunately, Alexander's uncle James bought them back for him. Alexander must have feasted on the contents—stories of Roman heroes and Greek philosophers, stories of war and peace.

Then their cousin Peter suddenly committed suicide. So the question remained—what was to happen to Alexander and James?

James was made an apprentice to a carpenter. Thomas Stevens, a merchant, and his wife, Ann, asked Alexander to live with them. And so he did. This was a happy period for Alexander, the first time he'd had a part in warm family life.

He became best friends with Edward, one of the Stevenses' sons. Edward was Alexander's age and the two boys shared many of the same dreams. Edward's upbringing had been different from Alexander's—his family was rich and respected—but he never allowed this difference to come between them. And Alexander often reminded Edward how lucky he was to have his advantages.

Alexander and Edward remained close friends, and when Edward left the West Indies to go to college in America, he and Alexander corresponded. Edward wrote about the growing unrest in America between the colonists and the British. Alexander wrote to Edward of all his dreams. He was daydreaming, he confessed, "building castles in the air," but he advised Edward not to tell this to his American friends, for they would only laugh. He ended up with his often-repeated wish—"I wish there was a war!" As far as he could see, war was the only way a poor boy could distinguish himself.

Alexander was working as a clerk for Nicolas Cruger in a trading company on St. Croix. Then Nicolas Cruger took sick and went back to New York, leaving Alexander, barely in his teens, in charge of the St. Croix office. There was no one else in the company available and Alexander had already proved himself to be mature and responsible. So Alexander took over, making decisions as needed and reporting by letter to his superiors. He managed several voyages, including that of the *Thunderbolt*, a ship that went to the Spanish Main (in central South America) to trade its cargo in exchange for a load of donkeys. This trip did not go well. The ship was late returning and when it finally did arrive, Alexander discovered that the donkeys were mostly sick or dead. He did what he could to save a few of the animals and didn't hesitate to take the ship's captain to task. What could that captain have thought, being scolded by such a young boy? When Cruger came back after a five-month absence, Alexander returned to his clerking responsibilities, having learned much more about commerce and how to deal with challenging situations.

It was not long after this, however, that something else occurred that changed Alexander's life. On August 31, 1772, when Alexander was seventeen, a terrible hurricane hit the West Indies.

It had a profound effect on everyone, including Alexander. It lasted six hours and was such a violent storm that houses were leveled, trees were toppled and ships at sea were overturned or reduced to sticks. It was fiercer than anything the people had experienced before.

On Sunday, preachers preached sermons, asking if the

hurricane was a punishment from God. Everyone was frightened, Alexander among them. But God had acted like this in the Old Testament, he told himself. "Why not now?"

Indeed, Alexander was so impressed he wrote a letter to his father, describing the hurricane in every detail. At one point he broke into his own descriptive style to express the terror he felt during the hurricane.

"Good God!" he wrote. "What terror and destruction! The roaring of the sea and the wind, fiery meteors flying about in the air. The prodigious glare of almost perpetual lightning, the crash of falling houses were sufficient to strike astonishment into angels."

Alexander had always taken pride in his ability to write.

Indeed, a couple of poems that he had written had been printed in the local newspaper. He must have shown his piece on the hurricane to Hugh Knox. Knox was a preacher who had become a close friend and something of a mentor to Alexander when he had shown an interest in religion. He asked Alexander if he could send his letter to the newspaper. The editor was so impressed by Alexander's writing that he published it. It received a great deal of attention. The result was that a number of local men offered to start a fund to send Alexander to college in America. Edward Stevens's father and his employer Nicolas Cruger were probably among them, since they already knew how bright Alexander was.

Another supporter of Alexander's education was his cousin Ann Lytton Venton, who was twelve years older than Alexander and with whom he had a special relationship. Ann Venton took an early interest in Alexander, and much later in life he remembered her as his "best friend." Ann had inherited a portion of her father James's estate after her brother Peter's suicide and her father's subsequent death. Ann had recently left for New York, entrusting Alexander with power of attorney to collect money due from the estate. This money may have helped finance Alexander's education.

Alexander was going to college in America! Nothing could have pleased him more. His benefactors gave him clothes suitable for a college student and a ticket on one of Cruger's coastal ships. The three-week voyage almost ended in catastrophe. On the approach to Boston harbor, flames appeared over the deck. The ship was on fire! Passengers were shouting in alarm and ship's officers were rushing about, giving orders. With great effort, the crew managed to put out the fire with buckets of seawater and the ship docked safely in Boston. Alexander made inquiries and found a nearby dock where a ship was about to leave for New York. When it left, Alexander was on it.

CHAPTER TWO

O nce in New York, Alexander went to Kortright and Company to pick up his allowance. They handled his education fund for the subscribers in St. Croix. Probably through a junior partner there, he met his first friend in New York, Hercules Mulligan, an enthusiastic, outgoing Irishman. He ran a tailor shop on the East Side and lived in rooms upstairs with his family. It is likely that Alexander boarded at the Mulligans' when he first arrived because he and Hercules became fast friends and remained so.

In 1773 New York, there was much talk of politics. Hercules was a political activist, an ardent patriot who seemed to know all the leaders on the patriot side. He was full of the kind of talk that Alexander loved to hear, like what actions England had recently been taking and how the colonies had responded. They talked about the British in New York and Hercules told him that it was mostly the Liberty Boys who had been acting up. Alexander had nothing good to say about the Liberty Boys. He liked a society that was governed by rules. Not like the Liberty Boys, who made up their own rules.

As soon as possible, Alexander went to see his old friend Edward Stevens at King's College. It was in an almost rural area north of the city and he felt at home right away. He liked the way the grass ran down to the North River (now the Hudson) and he was almost sorry he wasn't staying at King's.

But while he was still in St. Croix it had been decided that he should attend a preparatory school to study Latin, Greek and higher mathematics before he could go on to college. He was to go to the Elizabethtown Academy in New Jersey. Edward and his roommates hoped that Alexander would return from New Jersey and join them at King's. Alexander hoped so too, but he knew he had to start at Elizabethtown.

The academy consisted of two brick buildings topped by a cupola that were set on the grounds of a Presbyterian church and surrounded by rich farmland, just the way Alexander might have imagined it would be in England or Scotland.

One of the first things Alexander did upon arriving at the school was to present letters of introduction to two prominent men: Elias Boudinot, who would become president of the Continental Congress in 1782, and William Livingston, who later became the first governor of New Jersey in 1776. The letters were from Hugh Knox, who had known the men when he attended the College of New Jersey at Princeton. Alexander was pleased at the reception the men gave him and the friendship they offered. Never at a loss for conversation with men of importance, Alexander was soon at home in their households. Always interested in girls, he carried on a flirtation with young Catherine "Kitty" Livingston.

In addition to the regular course of study, Alexander decided to teach himself French. He had heard much about what the French philosophers thought of politics and wanted to read what they had to say in their own language. He had had some introduction to French—for he had heard his mother, who was of French Huguenot descent, speak it occasionally and perhaps had tried to speak it too. In any case, he started studying and by the end of the summer, Alexander had become fairly fluent in French and was much impressed with the French philosophers.

After six months, Alexander had finished his courses at Elizabethtown and was ready to apply to college. It is likely that he would have gone straight to King's, but his two benefactors, Livingston and Boudinot, were trustees at the College of New Jersey, so he felt obliged to apply there. He had an interview with the president of the college and told him he'd like to take his college courses at his own pace. He was anxious to move along as fast as he could. The president said that might be difficult. The Board of Trustees would have to decide, and they usually didn't make exceptions.

But there was Aaron Burr, Alexander pointed out. An exception had been made for him.

Aaron's father had been the president of the College of New Jersey. He had died there at age forty-five when Aaron was only nineteen months old. Alexander had heard how Aaron applied when he was eleven years old. He was turned down, but he studied hard for two years and was allowed to skip the first year and enter the sophomore class at age thirteen. Most students entered their first year at the age of fourteen or fifteen.

But there had been another exception, the president told him. James Madison had been admitted to the college and finished three years in just two. He completed his work satisfactorily, but at the end of the time he was so exhausted from the pressure that he became sick. The college decided it would be careful about making exceptions in the future.

In any case, Alexander was refused permission to advance on his own terms. So he did exactly what he had secretly wanted to do ever since he arrived in America. He went to New York and applied to King's with the same request that he might advance at his own pace. This was made easy for him when he found that instead of signing up for regular lectures, he could take private classes. Now he could go ahead faster. He could also, if he wished, become involved in politics.

Near the time that Alexander entered King's, a dramatic event took place in Boston on the evening of December 16, 1773. Two hundred men thought to be Liberty Boys boarded three British ships and threw 342 chests of tea into the harbor to protest the tax on tea as Bostonians cheered them on from the shore. Hercules Mulligan knew how Alexander felt about the Liberty Boys, so he reminded Alexander that the people of Boston had tried everything else first. And the Tea Party wasn't just the doing of the Liberty Boys. Some of the First Citizens of Boston had a hand in it too.

Alexander hadn't made up his mind about the conflict between England and America. But ever since he had arrived in America, this was all people talked about. Now that he was here, he might have to decide.

In political outlook, King's was more conservative than the College of New Jersey. King's favored the Tories, who were loyal to the English king, and the College of New Jersey favored the Whigs, who also called themselves patriots. But that didn't matter to Alexander. He was trying to see all sides.

Alexander enjoyed his friendship with his roommates. They liked this attractive, smart, accomplished young man from the West Indies. In time, he shared a room with his good friend Robert Troup, an upperclassman. Although his classmates attended church regularly, as was the custom, Alexander may have surprised them. For as Robert reported, Alexander dropped to his knees night and morning to say his prayers.

Indeed, life was far busier than Alexander had anticipated. Along with his studies, he and his roommates formed a private club in which they debated, questioned, and wrote papers that they submitted to each other for criticism. In the fall of 1774 he began reading articles (also called pamphlets) published by a Mr. Rivington, a political activist who printed pieces on both sides of the controversy between England and America. When Alexander read a long article signed A. W. Farmer, he decided he felt so strongly about it that he would answer it.

Obviously, the article called "A Westchester Farmer" was not written by a farmer, but by a Tory leader who wanted to get his views across. In his anonymous reply, Alexander accused him of flying under false colors—misrepresenting himself. What was more, A. W. Farmer was ignorant, he said. He talked of "natural rights," but didn't seem to know that every person had a God-given natural right. Everyone had a right to criticize his government. It was a high and mighty tone that nineteen-year-old Alexander used. And it attracted a great deal of attention as articles flew back and forth over the months.

But not everyone was limiting himself to writing propaganda. Just as Hercules Mulligan had said, the Liberty Boys were busy in New York. Sometimes their demonstrations turned violent.

On July 6, 1774, they gathered at the Liberty Pole on a grassy common near King's College where people with different views came to air their ideas publicly. They were calling for a boycott on British goods.

Alexander was there only as an observer. But as he listened, he was moved to go up onto the platform and express how he felt. He ended up giving a strong, passionate speech, explaining his fast-growing allegiance to the patriot argument.

When he finished speaking, people were stunned. "It's a collegian. It's a collegian," they whispered to each other in amazement. Although Alexander was nineteen, he looked even younger to them. Perhaps some had recognized him as the boy who talked to himself. He could be seen early in the morning walking the streets around King's, speaking aloud to himself. What he was actually doing was memorizing his lessons or his reading. He never had enough time to read, so he would get up early, read, then walk about, repeating what he'd read. He had done the same thing at Elizabethtown, but there he had walked in a deserted cemetery.

One night Alexander heard a commotion in the courtyard at King's. He looked out and saw the president of the college, Dr. Myles Cooper, leaning out his window in a long nightshirt, his wispy hair standing up like the ruffled comb of a rooster. A mob had broken down the gates to come after the president, a determined Tory, to tar and feather him and run him out of town.

Alexander raced down the steps and confronted the mob at the door, giving Dr. Cooper a chance to go out the back.

Dr. Cooper climbed over a fence and ran down the hill to the river where some English ships were moored. The next day Alexander was relieved to hear that Dr. Cooper had leaped aboard a ship and was on his way to England.

England didn't let up on the colonies. It kept imposing new laws aimed at keeping them in line. Public documents were to be taxed. A couple couldn't secure a marriage license without paying a tax. A troop of five hundred British soldiers was sent to Boston to keep order. They were to be quartered in colonial houses without the permission of the owners and were told they could enter and search the homes of colonists for any reason.

Of course such actions inflamed the citizens of Boston. When more troops arrived from England in late spring of 1775, a makeshift army of Boston citizens fought at Breed's Hill, north of Dorchester, and nearby Bunker Hill, determined to defend the city. It was such a fierce conflict that no one was sure what the outcome was until it was over. Over four hundred Americans had been killed or wounded, but one thousand British soldiers had gone down. Surely after this fight the British had gained respect for colonial power and the ability to defend its citizens.

How would England react? New York was sure it would be the next to feel its wrath. The Tories failed in a last-ditch effort to negotiate peace between England and America. They had persuaded the Second Continental Congress to send to London what they called the Olive Branch Petition.

And what happened? Nothing. England did not even acknowledge the petition. Instead, in August 1775, a huge British battleship, the *Asia*, sailed into New York harbor, bristling with cannons.

Americans knew that if the *Asia* proceeded very far, the city and all its buildings could be destroyed. New Yorkers would obviously have to do something. The alarm went out. Citizens responded, rushing to the Battery where the cannons were stored.

Alexander grabbed his musket and with fifteen other King's collegians raced off to pull the cannons up from the Battery and store them near the Liberty Pole on the Common. He was coming back when he met Hercules trying to pull a cannon with a rope. He told Hercules to hold his musket while he pulled the cannon up to safety. When he went back to get his musket, Alexander found that Hercules had dropped it in all the excitement.

By now the *Asia* had sent a smaller boat close to shore, where the British sailors on board were firing their own cannons. The thunder of the British cannons was overwhelming, but the many smaller cannons at New York's disposal created a cloud of fire and a series of holes in the *Asia*. As the men around him ran back to take cover, a cool, unconcerned Alexander stayed and looked for his musket.

Finally, musket in hand, Alexander found Hercules and they watched as the smaller boat retreated and the *Asia* was turning to leave the harbor.

Hercules looked at the cap Alexander was wearing—a round green cap that said "Liberty or Death"—and he guessed that Alexander had become a patriot at last.

Soldier

CHAPTER THREE

In the spring of 1775, Alexander had joined the "Corsicans," a group of young men who met regularly and drilled in St. Paul's churchyard. Alexander took his training seriously. He studied military history and its tactics with all the hard work and drive he put into his studies at King's.

George Washington had been appointed the commander in chief of the Continental army on June 15. Alexander saw him for the first time ten days later, when he came to New York on his way to Massachusetts. A carriage pulled by white horses carried him past King's College. Alexander must have been impressed with this distinguished-looking man who wore a fine purple sash across his blue uniform and a grand plumed hat atop his head.

Toward the end of the year, Alexander was busy writing revolutionary essays for a New York newspaper. When a mob broke into the print shop of Mr. Rivington, the editor who had published Alexander's anonymous essays in answer to the Tory leader "A. W. Farmer," Alexander wrote that their actions were "dangerous and pernicious." Mr. Rivington had moved more and more to the Tory way of thinking and Alexander considered him a contemptible man. But he despised mob violence even more.

In early 1776 Alexander McDougall, a Scot and a fierce patriot, was forming the first artillery regiment in New York. He may have known of Alexander through William Livingston. In any case, twenty-one-year-old Alexander was commissioned by McDougall to be Captain Alexander Hamilton of the New York Provincial Company of Artillery.

Captain Hamilton was not only responsible for recruiting men, but for supplying them with uniforms. Perhaps he turned to Hercules for advice. He must have been pleased when he saw his men lined up, dressed in blue jackets with buff collars and white shoulder straps fastened at the waist. He became known as an officer who wanted his soldiers well trained, disciplined and smartly dressed.

While Hamilton and his men were setting to work building a fort on Bayard's Hill in lower Manhattan, the Continental Congress was meeting in Philadelphia. They had decided it was no good to fight the British colony by colony, city by city. They would have to unite and fight together. They intended to break off from Great Britain and declare themselves a free and independent country. For some this was hard. How could they walk away from the king whom they had followed and obeyed—and yes, loved—for so long?

The delegates went home to think and to talk with the people. Twenty days later, they went back to Philadelphia to vote on whether or not to declare their independence.

Soon after the vote, which set the colonies on the path to independence, a group of distinguished-looking men were meeting and working on a document to accomplish that very thing. A committee of three men was appointed to write it—

John Adams, Thomas Jefferson and Benjamin Franklin. But in the end, they considered Jefferson the finest writer and gave the task to him. On July 2, 1776, the first draft was voted on and on July 4 the Congress approved the final document.

On that same July 2, Hamilton watched from the Battery as masses of ships under the command of General William Howe sailed into New York harbor to Staten Island, carrying thousands of British redcoats and German mercenaries, known as Hessians. There were so many ships that an eyewitness wrote, "I declare that I thought all London was afloat."

On July 9, General Washington and his soldiers stood at attention in the Commons below King's College to listen to the Declaration of Independence being read aloud.

"When in the course of human events," it began. At the end, everyone knew that the colonies were now a free and independent country. They cheered. Soldiers picked up their muskets and on the officer's signal pointed them to the sky and fired thirteen rounds, one for each of the thirteen states.

If this was now a free country, Alexander must have thought, he had helped make it so. But he also knew that the fight for freedom between the old country and the new was far from over. It was just beginning.

New York's citizens had waited a long time for the British

The Thirteen Colonies
IN 1775

Scale of miles

100   50   0   100   200

Extent of Settlement

to take some action against them. With the appearance of British ships, Hamilton, like everyone else, was tense with anticipation. The people of New York were afraid for their city and they continued to make preparations for its defense. They built trenches and more trenches. They barricaded the east-west streets of the city. And they waited.

Then, on July 12, Hamilton got a taste of British might. The *Phoenix,* a forty-four-gun battleship, and the *Rose,* a twenty-gun frigate, went up the river west of the city firing. Hamilton and his men manned four large cannons from the Battery. As they fired at the ships, one of the cannons exploded, killing two of his men. The *Phoenix* and the *Rose* continued upriver unchecked and eventually returned to port. It was a certain sign of British strength with the distinct purpose of putting fear into the Americans.

On July 14, ten days after America declared its independence, Great Britain tried to establish contact with the army under the command of General George Washington. On that day a small boat carrying a Lieutenant Brown and a flag of truce was sent by Lord Howe to Washington's headquarters on Wall Street. Americans had seen the boat approaching, as had Joseph Reed (one of Washington's best friends) and Henry Knox.

"Sir," Lieutenant Brown said, stepping ashore. "I have come to deliver a letter to George Washington."

Joseph Reed didn't hesitate a second. "We have no one in this army with that name," he said. Reed, like all Americans, resented the fact that the British refused to recognize that Washington was their commander in chief.

"By what title is he addressed?" Brown asked.

"You are very sensible that he is known as the general of the American army."

Lieutenant Brown tried to smooth things over but in the end returned to Lord Howe with the rejected letter.

Lieutenant Brown returned a second time with the letter. This time it was addressed to "George Washington, Esq., Esq., etc., etc."

Then a different representative was sent with the request that Washington receive the adjutant general. Washington agreed, and although it was a pleasant enough meeting, the adjutant general left the same letter behind him addressed to "George Washington, Esq., Esq., etc., etc." Washington would not even pick it up, so that was the end of all negotiations between the two countries.

A month later, General Washington knew that the danger was growing and he asked New Yorkers to evacuate their city. Out of the population of 25,000, about 5,000 stayed behind.

On the night of August 21, Hamilton and his men were in Fort Bayard when Colonel McDougall came in and told them to batten down the hatches—there was going to be a storm. Hamilton must have wondered if it might match that terrible hurricane on St. Croix. Gusts of wind were bending trees so low they looked as if they were bowing to a higher authority. At any other time Hamilton would have thought that the British were attacking. Thunder cracked and rolled like cannon fire. A group of people ran as if trying to escape the devil himself. Four or five others were struggling along the path below the fort, hugging the hillside as they went. Suddenly a huge lightning bolt enveloped in flames dropped from the sky, hesitated on the roof of the fort, then slid down the hill, striking and killing them. Hamilton was looking out as it happened. Perhaps he wondered if this were a sign of things to come.

The next day, on August 22, the invasion of Long Island got under way. Ninety British vessels could be seen in the Narrows. British troops and German mercenaries were packed into dozens of flatboats with British sailors at the oars. At the end of a few days, twenty thousand troops had reached Long Island.

American Loyalists with long-hidden supplies of food met the first wave of four thousand British and German soldiers who landed at Gravesend. As they headed toward Brooklyn, a Hessian soldier said, "Houses and fields in ashes, roads lined with dead cattle and old people looking with sadness at what had appeared previously to have been a paradise."

Retreating American soldiers had killed the cattle and set the houses on fire when the British landed.

For a week the Americans fought the British. Poorly trained, inexperienced and outnumbered, the Americans suffered heavy losses. Within a week, Washington and his army found themselves hemmed in between British forces and the East River. Washington decided that a stealthy nighttime retreat under cover of darkness was the only answer. They were

to take off their boots, remove blankets from their haversacks, and replace them with their boots. If they were wearing shoes, they were to tie them around their necks. They were to move slowly, in absolute silence, to the waterfront, where boats would take them to Manhattan.

Hamilton and others might have doubted this could be done. But they did it! The entire army moved silently across Brooklyn and down to the waiting boats. With their oars wrapped in blankets, men rowed back and forth across the river. At dawn, the retreat was still going on, but luckily a thick fog rolled in and hid those who were left. Hamilton and Washington were among the last men to cross.

Two weeks later British forces attacked at Kips Bay on the East River. The American soldiers flew in all directions, undisciplined and disorderly. George Washington on horseback was in this chaos of a crowd. Dismayed at what he saw, he shouted, "Are these the men with whom I am to defend America?"

As the army retreated out of the city and north to Harlem Heights, Hamilton and his men brought up the rear, trudging through the rain and dragging what artillery they had left. Tired and worn-out, they reached the Heights in the dark.

In late October, Washington ordered his army to head north again. After a long march they reached White Plains and found a large field where they set up camp. Washington had come to know Hamilton while they were at Harlem Heights and was impressed with his organizational skills and military knowledge. Hamilton was among the men he sent to Chatterton's Hill to stop any British trying to cross the shallow Bronx River below.

All too soon, Hamilton must have heard the martial music from his position on a rocky ledge. Preceded by a band, the British came on through the White Plains field, flags flying, with mounted cannons and a cavalry. They stopped at the foot of Chatterton's Hill and opened fire. The Americans returned fire.

As more British soldiers waded across the knee-deep water of the Bronx River, Hamilton began spraying the river, aiming with a constant shower of grapeshot. It seemed effective until the British suddenly turned and were no longer in range. Then they regrouped and stormed the hill, and Hamilton and the Americans had to retreat. Another defeat for the Americans, even though the British losses were greater.

Washington was clearly discouraged as he gave the order to cross the Hudson River to Fort Lee in New Jersey. From there he saw the enemy overrun Fort Washington on the opposite shore, and only days later they had to flee across New Jersey, leaving Fort Lee to the British.

It would be seven long years before Hamilton would see New York City again.

CHAPTER FOUR

The Americans headed for the King's Highway that led through New Jersey to Philadelphia. It was a long march, step after step, mile after mile. They had to keep a careful eye out for the British. They could be anywhere. At night, they slept in woods by the side of the road. When they were hungry (but not *too hungry,* Washington warned them), they stopped for food and drink at farmhouses, especially if they had seen some sign that they were the homes of patriots.

The Americans believed the British would want to capture Philadelphia next. Not many people were left in the city. Fearful of war, they had fled. The Continental Congress, which had made Philadelphia its headquarters, had moved to Baltimore in Maryland.

Washington was headed for the outskirts of Trenton, but once there he had to retreat to Pennsylvania to get away from the British. It was during this withdrawal that Washington saw Hamilton's cool courage under fire as he remained at the rear to provide cover for the Americans. He later commented that he "was charmed by the brilliant courage and admirable skill" of the young officer.

Washington set up an encampment across the river in Pennsylvania, north of Trenton. He was determined to return and fight the Hessians who occupied Trenton. His plan was to attack them on Christmas night. Unlike the British, who observed Christmas only as a religious day in the church calendar, the Hessians celebrated with lively traditional feasts and bouts of self-indulgence. A Christmas night attack would come as a surprise to them.

Washington, however, had all kinds of obstacles in his way before any attack could take place. His army had dwindled, both through desertions and sickness. General Greene described it as being "a shadow army." Many of his men were due to leave the army at the end of the year. And with so many defeats and poor living conditions, how could Washington motivate them to stay? And for those who did stay, how could he encourage them to fight? And where was General Charles Lee, who was expected to join the attack with four thousand soldiers?

On December 3, the answer came. General Lee was nearby, but he had stopped at a tavern in Basking Ridge. There he made himself comfortable in his dressing gown and slippers and was going over some papers when a scouting party of British soldiers, led by the daredevil British officer Banastre Tarleton, burst into the tavern, arrested Lee and took him off as a prisoner.

Washington was furious when he heard of Lee's injudicious behavior, but even more so when Lee's army began drifting into the American headquarters at a local farmhouse. Of the four thousand troops expected, only half were fit to fight a battle. A large number appeared to be in such ragged condition that they were completely unprepared for what might lie ahead.

Hamilton was ill in bed the day before the attack on Trenton. But at five o'clock the following evening he was there on the riverbank, ready to cross the Delaware to fight. He made the icy crossing in the boat carrying Washington.

Twenty-four hundred men made it across the river, but they were late arriving because of the terrible weather. They had planned to get there between midnight and three in the morning. Instead they started marching toward Trenton at four a.m. and the Hessians realized they were coming.

Washington led the way against the Hessians, who had gathered along two main streets of the town. Seeing the size of the attack, the Hessians ducked into side streets with the Americans at their heels. Snow, however, had so dampened the muskets of the Americans that they were no longer able to fire them.

"What should we do?" a soldier called out to Washington. "We can't fire our muskets."

Washington didn't hesitate. "Then use your bayonets!" he snapped.

For a moment all that could be heard was the sound of bayonets being unlocked from the "hold" positions on their muskets. Then there was the awful crunch of bodies meeting their targets. Like the rest of the army, Hamilton was used to bayonet practice on the safe confines of an army field. He had once said, "war is a dirty business." He must have thought so that night.

Suddenly, the Hessians took control of one of their cannons and turned it on the Americans. But two brave American officers rushed up—Captain William Washington and Lieutenant James Monroe. They grabbed the cannon from the Hessians and turned it on them. The Hessians retreated and the battle was over—a stunning victory for the Americans, who lost only two men. And they had frozen to death. Five had been wounded, among them William Washington and James Monroe. Out of the 1,500 Hessians, 21 were killed, 90 were wounded, and 896 were taken prisoner. The Americans captured six horses and six cannons, plus muskets, ammunition, a drum and other instruments from the Hessian marching band.

The following day, Washington drew his army around him. He congratulated them on this excellent performance and promised each of those who had crossed the Delaware a bounty of ten dollars to be drawn from the sale of all captured

Hessian goods. A bounty of ten dollars would have seemed a considerable sum of money to soldiers whose monthly pay was six dollars. Shoes from the dead Hessians, much needed by the Americans, were distributed to the men.

In early January, General Cornwallis and his men arrived, attacking the Americans at Assunpink Creek, just south of Trenton. As it got dark, both sides pulled back for the night and a British general commented to General Cornwallis, "If I know Washington, he won't be there in the morning."

Cornwallis paid no attention, and by morning, of course, Washington was gone. Counting on surprise as he so often did, Washington and his army had crept silently away at night, leaving a contingent of men to build campfires and make the appropriate sounds of a large army to fool the enemy.

Instead of going in the direction that the British expected, Washington's men made a wide sweep, arriving at the rear of the college at Princeton. It was not long before the Americans and the British were exchanging fire again. The battle grew more fierce and continued in the large open fields of William Clarke's nearby farm. General Hugh Mercer, a close friend of Washington's, had his horse shot out from under him. Surrounded by British soldiers, he bravely tried to fight them off with his saber but was stabbed seven times and left for dead.

An officer wrote that the sight of Washington in battle set an example of courage that the men had never seen before. "Parade with us, my brave fellows," Washington is said to have called out to them. "There is but a handful of the enemy, and we will have them directly."

They did. And they proceeded to the front of the college, where the fighting continued. Hamilton and others broke down the doors of the college. The British came streaming in after them. Hamilton was among the men who turned and shot at the British until they rushed back outside. The Americans followed, shooting all the way.

No one can say for sure, but the story goes that Hamilton was just outside the windows of the college chapel when he noticed a portrait of King George II hanging on the wall. He wheeled his cannon into position in the college yard, aimed and fired. The portrait shattered and the head of George II fell to the floor.

Thanks to the battles at Trenton and Princeton, Philadelphia was not captured by the British. It gave Washington time to regroup and move his army to Morristown, where they would spend the winter. And it gave the soldiers the encouragement they needed to go on after so many defeats.

On January 20, 1777, General Washington wrote to Captain Hamilton, asking him to join his staff as an aide-de-camp. Hamilton had already turned down similar invitations from both General Greene and Lord Stirling. Most young men of twenty-two would have been thrilled to be selected to join Washington's staff, but not Hamilton. He thrived on the excitement of battle. The last thing he wanted was to be behind a desk writing letters, even if they were for the commander in chief of the Continental army. Still, how could he say no?

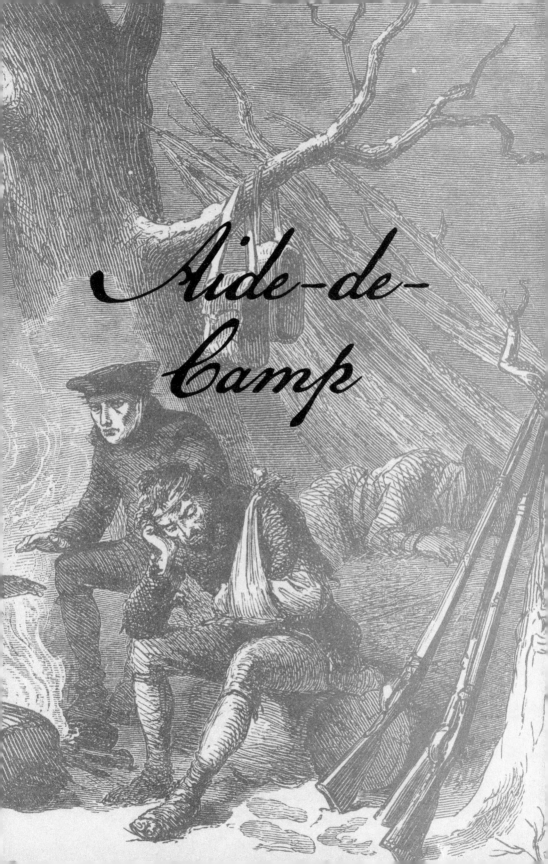

Aide-de-camp

CHAPTER FIVE

lthough Hamilton had mixed feelings about accepting Washington's offer, he had intense admiration for him. So on March 1, 1777, he was officially appointed aide-de-camp and promoted to lieutenant colonel. It was not the field command he wanted, but he hoped that in time Washington would give him more responsibility, take him into his confidence and ask his advice. Hamilton never doubted his ability to do anything that was asked of him. He gradually came to appreciate the fact that Washington had equal confidence in him—not only in Hamilton's ability to write letters for his signature, but to write them as if

Washington had dictated them himself. Perhaps in private recognition of Hamilton's pride, as well as his ability, Washington gave him an assignment to report to Congress on the reorganization of the army.

The army had moved into its new winter quarters in Morristown, New Jersey. As a member of Washington's "family," Hamilton enjoyed the company of the other aides, particularly John Laurens of South Carolina, who became his close friend almost from the moment they met. Alexander felt that he and John had been cut from the same cloth. John was his intellectual equal, and Alexander admired his "zeal, intelligence, enterprise."

In July 1777 the Americans defeated the British under General John Burgoyne at Saratoga in upstate New York, a major strategic victory. General Horatio Gates was acknowledged the victor at Saratoga, although Alexander and many others felt that General Benedict Arnold, with his daring exploits, should be given the credit.

One of the results of Saratoga was a strong backlash that developed against Washington. After all, Saratoga under Gates had been a major victory in the war, but aside from the battle of Trenton against the Hessians, Washington didn't have much to show for his leadership. So a group of conniving men gathered around Gates, lobbying that he be made commander in chief.

In October 1777, Washington sent Colonel Hamilton to Albany to meet General Gates and tell him to send much-needed troops to Morristown to augment Washington's dwindling army. This difficult assignment once again demonstrated Washington's recognition of Hamilton's ability.

If Hamilton was pleased with this mission, Gates was not. It was clear from the way he acted, more than from what he said, that Gates considered Alexander Hamilton unsuitable to deal with such an experienced man as himself. Gates not only outranked him, he saw Hamilton as being young and cocky. In the end, Gates did send Washington a small number of ill-equipped soldiers, but it was far from the sizeable numbers that Washington had been expecting.

Still, Hamilton could not have felt his trip to Albany was a waste of time. He was invited to dinner at the home of General Philip Schuyler. There he met twenty-year-old Elizabeth "Eliza" Schuyler, the daughter of the general. As he later described her, she was the personification of everything that Alexander found desirable in a woman.

On his way home from Albany, Hamilton took sick with a fever and rheumatic pains. When he was well enough to move on, he took sick again and returned by coach to Peekskill, where the doctor ordered him to bed to fully recover, which took more time than everyone expected.

By the time Hamilton reached Morristown, it was January and Washington had moved the army headquarters to Valley Forge, Pennsylvania, west of Philadelphia. Compared to Morristown, Valley Forge was a disorganized mess. The huts were only half built, the roofs leaked, and rainwater that stood in puddles turned into deep, deep mud, making it unfit for wagons to move. It was almost impossible for men to walk, especially in bare or rag-covered feet (many still had no shoes). The only warmth they had was from huddling around campfires.

Hamilton was upset at the conditions he found at Valley Forge. In fact, in frustration he wrote to George Clinton, the newly elected governor of New York, expressing his disgust at

Congress's lack of action and wondering what branch of government could help the army. But letters were not enough.

There were, however, several sources of distraction for the army. One was the daily drill that Baron Friedrich von Steuben, a crack drillmaster from Germany, conducted. He and Hamilton became good friends, even though the baron was considerably older. They shared a love of the military and a disci-plined army. And Hamilton spoke French and could translate for him. "The baron is a gentleman for whom I have particular esteem," Hamilton said.

Steuben had volunteered to get the American army in shape for fighting, and he was making this happen. The men put up with his incessant drilling, and Steuben's habit of sprinkling his orders with colorful oaths—both in German and English—made them like him all the more.

Another source of entertainment was singing. Especially popular at Valley Forge was the song that, during the French and Indian War, General Wolfe had composed in Quebec on the night before he died. It had a sprightly tune and the words expressed the sentiments of the soldiers exactly.

> *How stands the glass around?*
> *For shame ye take no care, my boys.*
> *How stands the glass around?*
> *Let mirth and wine abound.*
> *(Repeat)*
> *The trumpets sound*
> *The colors they are flying, boys.*
> *To fight, kill or wound,*
> *May we still be found*
> *Content with our hard fare, my boys,*
> *On the cold ground.*

Perhaps the most popular form of distraction was reading aloud works by Thomas Paine. Washington had hoped that the entire army would hear Paine's *Common Sense,* and most of them did. Thomas Paine wrote in a Philadelphia newspaper, "This is the time for all good men to come to the aid of their country," and he went on ringing the call to renewed conviction, a willingness to sacrifice, and an uncompromising effort to win the freedom of the country. Paine's words were meant to be a rallying cry to America, and for many they were. They were meant to inspire courage in men whose spirits had been dulled by war. The men listened with undivided attention and at the end of the reading they often burst spontaneously into General Wolfe's song, so popular with the soldiers.

The winter of 1778 gave way to spring, and spring to summer, and both armies began moving again. In June the British general Clinton decided to move a large contingent of nine thousand men out of Philadelphia to New York. The British had occupied the city since September of 1777. With fifteen hundred wagons carrying supplies, they were forced to move slowly through New Jersey. Washington saw this as an opportunity to attack, even if some of his officers disagreed with him, especially General Charles Lee. He had been a prisoner of war ever since he'd been caught in Basking Ridge, but he had just been released in a prisoner exchange.

Washington first put the Marquis de Lafayette in charge of the advance army. But when Lee complained that he was the senior officer, Washington gave it to him. Washington's officers were skeptical about his choice and warned each other to watch Lee for any suspicious moves. Hamilton was also there, acting as a liaison officer to Lafayette. They were up front with Lee and determined to keep a close watch.

On June 27, the British soldiers camped near the Monmouth County Courthouse for the night. Lee was under orders to attack them the next morning. Washington was three miles behind with the main section of the army waiting for the attack to begin so he could move forward.

Soon after attacking as ordered, General Lee ordered the Americans to retreat. Hamilton shouted to Lee, "I will stay here with you, my dear general, and die with you! Let us all die rather than retreat!" But Lee wouldn't listen.

As soon as Washington heard what was happening, he galloped to the front and faced Lee.

"What is the meaning of this?" he demanded.

"The American troops would not stand the British bayonets," Lee told Washington.

Now Washington gave way to his temper. "You damned poltroon, you never tried them!"

The Americans stood rooted to the ground, transfixed by the sight of their calm general losing his temper. On and on Washington went, threatening to court-martial him. So he persisted, it was said, "till the leaves shook on the trees." When he had exhausted his vocabulary, Washington sent Lee to the rear and went to the front to lead the army in a charge.

The men plunged forward with new will, empowered to fight as they never had before—as if Thomas Paine himself had lit a fire under their feet. On this blistering hot day, the men dropped their shirts and jackets as they ran, bare to the waist. The sun beat down on their shoulders, but General Washington had insisted they fight. And fight they did.

No one, not even Washington, could remember such a fierce struggle as they fought their way through the day. It didn't seem like a single day, however. It didn't even seem like time as they knew it. It was as if eternity had dropped down and they were struggling through it. Hamilton had his horse shot from under him and, injured, he had to be carried from the field. Once again, as in previous battles, he had shown his cool determination in the face of danger.

At last the rays of the sun were shortening and the men realized that the day was over. The British disappeared into nearby woods. The Americans flung themselves to the ground in exhaustion. Hamilton's injuries had been attended to and now he rejoined Washington and Lafayette. They sat beneath a sheltering tree, hanging jackets on its branches. From the rear, wagons lumbered up with food. Two young boys handed Washington flasks of cold cider and a large basket of food. They were too tired to talk, so they ate quietly and then lay down to rest. Soon they were fast asleep.

Still, the battle wasn't over for everyone. Eventually Lee faced a court-martial and was found guilty. His punishment was suspension from the army for one year. But this didn't stop Lee from wandering around, filling the air with oaths and castigating Washington whenever anyone would listen.

John Laurens seemed to find Lee's behavior particularly offensive. He begged Hamilton to write something publicly against Lee, but Hamilton wouldn't do it. After all, he had testified against him in the court-martial. Laurens decided to take action on his own. He challenged Lee to a duel and asked Alexander to be his second. Lee accepted the challenge and a place and time were arranged.

In a wood near Philadelphia, Charles Lee and John Laurens faced each other. The order was given: "Present!" They aimed and fired. There is no evidence that Hamilton advised

Laurens to fire low, but Laurens did aim low. His bullet grazed Lee's thigh without inflicting any harm. But it was enough to scare Lee. Everyone thought the duel should continue, but Lee wanted to back out.

"I have never thought, nor did I say anything against Washington, the man. I esteem Washington," Lee said.

Hamilton nodded to Laurens. The duel was over.

CHAPTER SIX

n the meantime, Great Britain was not being idle. Turn-
ing its attention to the south, it was threatening Savannah,
Georgia, and would soon move to South Carolina, John
Laurens's home state. He resigned as an aide to Washington in
January 1779 so he could return home to help in its defense.

Hamilton wrote to Laurens often and some of his most
pessimistic letters date from this period. "I am disgusted
with everything in this world but yourself and *very* few more
honest fellows," he wrote, "and I have no other wish than as
soon as possible to make a brilliant exit. 'Tis a weakness, but
I feel I am not fit for this terrestreal [*sic*] country." In another

letter Hamilton wrote, "I hate Congress—I hate the army—I hate the world—I hate myself."

Among Hamilton's disappointments was the failure of a plan that Laurens had developed to recruit a black battalion into the army of South Carolina. Both Laurens and Hamilton were vehemently opposed to slavery. Hamilton sent a letter to Congress expressing his belief that slaves would make especially good soldiers with their training under Laurens and asking for their support, although he told Laurens, "I wish it success, but my hopes are very feeble." Congress did pass a resolution, but when Laurens asked for the approval of the South Carolina legislature, he was turned down, just as Hamilton had feared.

This was not the only opposition to Hamilton at the time. A congressman questioned his patriotism—how could a foreigner, an outsider, really care about America? Hamilton would face this charge from his critics all of his life.

The army spent the winter of 1780 camped in Morristown, New Jersey. Here there was an unexpected, but happy, distraction for Alexander. In February, Eliza Schuyler came to visit her aunt Gertrude, who was married to Washington's private doctor. When he had first met her in Albany, Alexander had liked her but had not been seriously impressed with her. All that changed.

On this longer visit, Alexander fell in love with Eliza and she with him. It became obvious to everyone one night at dinner. One of the aides remarked, "Hamilton is a gone man." Later he wrote that Eliza was "a brunette with the most good-natured, lively dark eyes I ever saw. . . ."

In March, Alexander proposed and Eliza accepted. With the uncertainty of the war always present, they began to tentatively plan a December wedding at the Schuyler home in Albany.

In whatever spare time he had, Hamilton worked on the economic problems that would face a country that was just starting out on its own. How would it repay the national debt, which was largely due to the war, and, even more challenging, how should it organize public finances? He went so far as to send a confidential six-thousand-word letter proposing his ideas to a member of Congress. He believed strongly in the creation of a central bank for the whole country, which would be owned by the government and private investors equally. The bank would print money and make loans. He wrote that the country would have to borrow a large amount of money from foreign countries, just the way the French and the British raised money during wartime.

Then in August the British attacked Camden, South Carolina, and a battle of some consequence took place. The fighting was so fierce that American officers ran away from the battle, with General Horatio Gates outrunning them all. Whatever reputation Gates had enjoyed before this, he lost now. There was no longer any talk of his replacing Washington as commander in chief.

Toward the end of the summer, Washington asked Hamilton and Lafayette to accompany him on a trip to Hartford, Connecticut, to confer with General Rochambeau, who had recently arrived from France with his army. After the meeting in Hartford, Washington wanted to go to West Point to meet with General Benedict Arnold, who was in charge. Arnold had become the West Point commandant that summer. It was later learned that he had deliberately not kept up the defenses of the fort to give the British an advantage.

Hamilton and another aide, James McHenry, rode ahead to the former home of Beverly Robinson, a prominent Tory, where Arnold was staying. While at breakfast with Hamilton and McHenry, Arnold received a dispatch, ran upstairs

to his wife, then rushed out of the house and down to the river, where he jumped into a boat.

Washington arrived shortly thereafter and went across to West Point to find General Arnold, but he wasn't there. Washington went back to the Robinson house, wondering where Arnold was. They waited.

Later in the afternoon, a messenger arrived with a packet of papers for Washington, inform-  ing him that a British officer, Major John André, dressed in civilian clothes and posing as "John Anderson," had been captured in Tarrytown, New York. He had in his possession a map of West Point. Washington turned to his aides. "Arnold has betrayed us! Whom can we trust now?"

They all looked downriver. Arnold must have rowed south. Washington told Hamilton and McHenry to get on their horses and ride after him. Before Washington had finished giving the order, Hamilton was astride his horse, galloping south beside the river. Too late. Arnold had boarded the British warship *Vulture* and was on his way down to British-occupied New York.

Back at the Robinson house, Hamilton went upstairs to

find Mrs. Arnold in the bedroom she shared with General Arnold. She was sitting on the bed, the pins out of her hair, which was disheveled and hanging down to her shoulders. She was holding her baby and crying uncontrollably.

"Washington is here," she cried. "He'll take my baby from me. He will take my baby away." She kept repeating herself over and over. Hamilton tried to calm her, but she wouldn't listen, so he went in search of Washington to report on Mrs. Arnold's condition.

Washington seemed concerned and went upstairs to see Mrs. Arnold himself. He sat upon the bed and tried to calm her down. He told her that Mr. Robinson would see that she was taken with her baby to her father's home in Philadelphia. Only later did Washington and Hamilton realize that Mrs. Arnold had been putting on an act to protect herself and her husband.

Major John André was taken to Tappan, New York, where his trial would take place. In a short time, André proved to be so likable, so brave, that none of the American officers could bear to think of what would happen to him, obviously a spy.

There was only one thing to do, Washington said, looking so pained that it was clear he meant to have André hanged. Hamilton told André what to expect at the outcome of his trial. André asked to be shot as a soldier, not hanged as a spy. Hamilton tried for a second time to convince Washington to let André be shot, but Washington only shook his head.

Later, when he saw the gallows, André said, "I am reconciled to my death, though I detest the mode."

Washington was with Hamilton, Henry Knox and Lafayette in a house not far from the gallows. No one had any intention of looking out the windows. Still, Washington ordered all the blinds to be drawn, and out of respect for André, whom he could not save, he stayed inside.

Hamilton returned to New Jersey, still affected by André's fate. He wrote to Eliza about his admiration for André. "I know I have talents and a good heart, but why am I not handsome? Why have I not every acquirement that can embellish human nature? Why have I not fortune, that I might hereafter have more leisure than I shall have to cultivate those improvements for which I am not entirely unfit?"

Hamilton spent much of his time writing letters. Since the wedding in Albany was to take place in several weeks, letters flew back and forth between Eliza and Alexander. He wrote to John Laurens and talked about his immediate future. He was marrying into a family with money, but as soon as the war was over, he intended to move with Eliza into a home of their own.

Hamilton's future father-in-law, General Schuyler, expressed the hope that after his marriage Hamilton would not be so ambitious. Hamilton was keeping busy writing political pieces, as well as studying law in every spare moment. Perhaps the general was making a diplomatic suggestion that Hamilton should not throw his weight around over every political controversy. Hamilton said he intended to lead a quiet life. But how could he make such a promise when he believed so passionately that he should speak his mind whenever the country's welfare was at stake?

In late November, Hamilton traveled to Albany for the wedding, which was to take place on December 14. On the appointed day, carriages pulled up in front of the Schuyler mansion. Twenty-five-year-old Alexander and twenty-three-year-old Eliza were married in the southeast parlor before her family and the prominent, wealthy upstate families, friends of the Schuylers. Of course there was no family there for Alexander, and because of the war only one of his army friends could attend. The others were all off on assignments. Sometime later, General and Mrs. Washington gave a reception for the newly married couple.

In January 1781, Alexander and Eliza joined the Washingtons in New Windsor, New York. Washington was confronting a potential widespread insurrection because soldiers were demanding back pay. Finally, the uprisings in Pennsylvania and New Jersey were quelled and the leaders were hanged.

But Washington remained tense and on edge. In February, he stood at the top of the stairs in his headquarters as Hamilton was going down. He asked to speak to him. Hamilton greeted him and explained that he was on his way downstairs to deliver a letter, but he would be right back. He was gone no more than a few minutes after stopping to speak briefly to Lafayette about some business. When he returned upstairs, however, he found Washington in a furor. "You have kept me waiting these ten minutes," he said. "I must tell you, sir, you treat me with disrespect!"

Hamilton could scarcely believe Washington's anger, which he felt was entirely unjustified. Not only had Washington's temper been aroused, his pride had obviously been touched. Well, Hamilton had a temper and pride too. He turned on his heel. "Then we must part," he said, and there was finality to his words.

When he told Lafayette about the exchange, Lafayette agreed that Hamilton had not been gone anywhere near ten minutes. Still he advised Hamilton to apologize to Washington. Eliza gave her husband the same advice. But Hamilton was stubborn. He had nothing to apologize for, he insisted. His sudden decision to leave may have been in part because of Washington's continued refusal to let him have a field command. But Hamilton had always disliked what he called the "personal dependence" of an aide-de-camp, and Washington's manner that day seemed like the final straw.

During the spring of 1781, Hamilton was being considered by a member of Congress for the position of superintendent of finance. When asked his opinion, Washington said that he had never talked about finance with Hamilton, so Congress subsequently offered the job to wealthy Robert Morris, a former congressman from Philadelphia. When Hamilton heard this, he wrote a long letter to Morris outlining his ideas, including the establishment of a national bank. At the same time, he wrote a series of essays called *The Continentalist* in which he described his ideas for a strong central government.

Hamilton continued to entreat Washington for a field command. In July 1781, at army headquarters in Dobbs Ferry, New York, Washington finally gave Hamilton command of a light infantry unit. Hamilton was pleased and surprised but wondered when he might see action. He was unaware of any fighting nearby. He hoped there would be an engagement in New York because Eliza was expecting their first child (he told her he wanted a boy) and Alexander wanted to be close by.

Then, in late September, Hamilton was sent by Washington to join Lafayette and John Laurens at Williamsburg to lay siege to Yorktown, where Cornwallis had his army. Hamilton was overjoyed to be with his friends again.

One day in early October, as he and Lafayette were standing near the British positions at Yorktown, Hamilton looked up and there coming down the hill was General Washington with his army. The British under Cornwallis had built ten earthen redoubts to protect their position. Numbers nine and ten were close to the American lines and the most vulnerable. Washington told the French army to take one redoubt and Lafayette could lead the Continental army into the other. Lafayette, in turn, appointed his aide to command his charge.

Hamilton wanted that command and requested that Washington give it to him. He was the senior officer, he insisted. Washington agreed and Hamilton returned to his tent, shouting, "We have it! We have it!"

On the night of October 14, Hamilton and his men charged the redoubt with bayonets only, as Washington had ordered. Hamilton ran across the open ground shouting war whoops as he dove into the redoubt. It was so shallow that Hamilton could feel only the arms and legs of the men that felt like large snakes on the ground. He flailed at them with his bayonet and with his open hands. The British were overcome. Some were carried out; most were captured. In the end, Hamilton emerged from the redoubt, looked across and saw Lafayette. They greeted each other quickly, walked together to Washington and saluted.

When it came time later for the formal surrender ceremony, the Americans and British soldiers lined up facing each other. Because Cornwallis was said to be sick, a British officer representing him carried the ceremonial sword of surrender and presented it to Rochambeau, who shook his head and

nodded toward Washington. The officer went to Washington, but Washington also shook his head and nodded toward General Benjamin Lincoln, who stood at the end of the line. Everyone knew that earlier in the war, Benjamin Lincoln, with a brigade of black soldiers from Massachusetts, had fought the British fiercely in Charleston, South Carolina, only to be forced to surrender. This was Washington's attempt to recognize Lincoln and his brigade's courage at Charleston.

There was a general feeling that the war was over now. Hamilton, however, knew that it would take more than the surrender at Yorktown to end the war. He was right.

It would be two more years before it finally ended. And even after Evacuation Day on November 25, 1783, when the British sailed out of New York harbor as the Americans replaced the Union Jack with their new flag, Washington feared the return of the British.

Statesman

CHAPTER SEVEN

After Yorktown, Alexander went immediately to Albany to be with Eliza for the birth of their first child. Their son was born on January 22, 1782. They named him Philip after Eliza's father.

Hamilton resigned from the army in March and stayed in Albany to study law. Because he had served in the war, he didn't have to do the required three-year apprenticeship under a lawyer and could work at his own pace. That May, before he took the bar exam in July, Robert Morris, the superintendent of finance, asked twenty-seven-year-old Hamilton to be the tax receiver for New York. Hamilton may have been reluctant to take on the job, since he was studying for his law exam and it paid little money. Still, Morris was an important person and they shared ideas on finance, such as the importance of a central bank. So he accepted. It led to interaction with the state legislators, who liked him, and Hamilton was named a New York delegate to the Continental Congress that would meet in Philadelphia the coming November.

In August, John Laurens was killed in South Carolina. Laurens, with a small group of soldiers, had intended to ambush a much larger British force near Charleston. But the British were warned that they were coming and hid in tall grass to wait for them. At the right moment they attacked the Americans and John Laurens was cut down in the heat of battle.

Washington was not surprised when he heard how Laurens died. He was sorry to hear about his former aide-de-camp's death, but he commented that Laurens's failing had always been that he was too rash and reckless.

Alexander was inconsolable. He and John had shared the same ideas and ideals for America. Moreover, Alexander was able to show John every side of himself, to tell him all his thoughts and feelings, as he was not able to do with anyone else. As much as Alexander loved Eliza, she didn't quite take the close place that John Laurens had.

As usual, however, life had practical matters, such as his Albany law practice, that had to be attended to. In November, Hamilton traveled to Philadelphia as a delegate from New York. There he met James Madison of Virginia for the first time. He found that they shared similar views about their new country, such as the importance of a central government with a national army (not just state militias) and the authority to raise taxes (and not depend upon the states to contribute money when they felt like it).

With the war over, the army was demanding back pay owed to them. In February, Hamilton suggested to Governor George Clinton that he set aside a portion of land for every officer and soldier who became a New York citizen. Clinton agreed.

In the meantime, officers in the army camp at New Windsor, New York, were on the verge of insurrection because they had not been paid, some for as long as six years. They had large debts waiting for them when they returned to their homes. It was Hamilton who persuaded General Washington to visit the camp and talk to the men.

Washington went in March 1783. He called the men together and took out a letter to read to them, but it all became a blur before his eyes.

"Gentlemen, you will permit me to put on my spectacles, for I have not only grown gray, but almost blind in service to my country." With a certain degree of shame, the men dropped their eyes. There was no more talk of insurrection over back pay that day.

But New York was not the only state to have dissatisfied soldiers. Many in Pennsylvania had reached the boiling point. A contingent of soldiers from Lancaster surrounded meeting rooms of the Congress and carried on in such a wild way that Congress determined to leave Philadelphia, fearing for its safety when the state militia did nothing. This was just the kind of mob action that Hamilton had always despised.

The Congress moved to the College of New Jersey, site of the battle of Princeton, but the quarters there were not large enough for the congressmen. They would move to Annapolis, Maryland; Trenton, New Jersey; and New York City before finally returning to Philadelphia in 1785. Out of this experience came the decision that one day the country would have a capital city in a special district all its own. It would not be part of any state.

In December the Hamiltons moved to New York and rented a house on Wall Street. Hamilton soon had a successful practice, even though he was sometimes criticized for the people he defended. With peace apparently so near, not only did soldiers want to go home, but Tories who had run off to England were coming back, expecting to occupy their old homes, and seeking damages for property that had been destroyed. They often sought restitution through the law and Hamilton was willing to take on their cases. It was not a popular thing to do, but Hamilton had never let popularity decide his course. It was, he thought, the right thing to do and that was what interested him.

At about the same time, Aaron Burr and his family moved into a house on the opposite end of Wall Street from the Hamiltons. Hamilton had gotten to know Burr in Albany, where he, too, had studied and practiced law. They had a mutual friend in Robert Troup, Hamilton's roommate at King's, so they saw each other socially. Hamilton once said that even though they had opposite views on politics, they were on good terms. In temperament, the two men were very different too. Burr was naturally secretive, while Hamilton was open. Burr rarely committed anything to writing; Hamilton, however, was not as careful. Even so, they occasionally worked together on legal cases.

Not all the immediate concerns of citizens could be handled right away, but as time passed, some people began to look ahead and wonder what kind of country did they want the United States of America to become? It was clear to a few, including Hamilton, that the Articles of Confederation, under which they had been operating, would not be adequate forever. The federal government did not have the power to tax. And even if America declared it was at war, how could it go ahead and fight with only state militias to depend on? Washington and Hamilton had too often been discouraged by a militia's refusal to fight when its enlistment time ended.

It would take until 1787 for Congress to meet in Philadelphia to talk about amending the Articles of Confederation. They were obviously thinking about writing a constitution, but they didn't call it a constitution at first. The discussions among the fifty-five delegates were private, with listeners stationed at closed doors to catch anything that might slip out. Benjamin Franklin, who loved to talk, was the one the delegates most worried about. No one wanted the country to know that they were considering a constitution until they were ready with a final document. Although many suggested plans, Edmund Randolph of Virginia came up with what he called the "Virginia Plan," which divided the government into three branches: the legislative, the executive, and the judiciary. The plan's design had representation in two legislative houses based on a state's population. The smaller states opposed this and William Paterson of New Jersey proposed one legislative house with equal representation by all states.

Hamilton, who had not spoken for a while, suddenly spoke at length, offering suggestions of his own, including that of an "elective monarch," as he chose to call him, who would serve for a life term or "during good behavior." *Monarch* was an unfortunate choice of words because it reminded everyone of George III, but Hamilton meant it to reflect his idea of the need for a strong leader. Above all, Hamilton feared that the democracy would deteriorate to a "mobocracy." Hamilton also had strong objections to any requirement that members of congress had to be native born or have lived in the country for a period of time. But he lost that fight. They did not have to be born in America, but senators had to live in the country for at least nine years and representatives for seven years. The president, they said, had to be native born. This must have hurt Hamilton, the obvious "outsider," and perhaps he sought to make a correction. The final version of the Constitution added that a person had to be native born or a citizen of the United States at the time of the adoption of the Constitution. No one rose to argue Hamilton's specific points, but not surprisingly, he had a hard time escaping the long-term effects of his use of the word *monarch*.

After much discussion, Roger Sherman of Connecticut proposed a compromise between the plans already presented. It was agreed that the House of Representatives would reflect each state's population and that two senators would equally represent each state in the Senate.

When it came time to sign the Constitution, only Alexander Hamilton's name appears representing New York State. Yates and Lansing Jr., the other two delegates from New York, had left early when they realized that the convention would be about more than amending the Articles of Confederation. It would take nine states to ratify the Constitution to make it legal.

Hamilton realized that the country, especially his home state of New York, needed to be persuaded to ratify the Constitution. To be persuaded, they needed to understand

it. He asked James Madison and John Jay to write a series of essays along with him. They would be printed in
newspapers under the common pseudonym of "Publius."
These essays, known collectively as *The Federalist,* were
an eloquent argument for the acceptance of the Constitution. There would be eighty-five essays in all—fifty-one by
Hamilton, twenty-nine by Madison and five by Jay, who fell
sick and had to stop writing.

When New Yorkers met in Poughkeepsie to deliberate
the ratification of the Constitution, Governor Clinton led a
group of upstate men opposed to it. Hamilton almost single-
handedly defended the federalist position against those
who felt the country was too big for one government and
who feared the total loss of states' rights. It was a fierce
struggle, and Hamilton deserves the credit for pulling New
York along. Even so, the vote on July 26, 1788, was tight—
30 to 27.

The outcome was not popular with upstate New York
voters, but New York City artisans, or tradesmen, were
ecstatic. They put on a big celebration with a parade down
Broadway. Hamilton was still in Poughkeepsie, but how
proud he must have been when he heard about it and the
grand twenty-seven-foot reproduction of a frigate called

The Hamiltonian—with flags flying in the breeze. In their enthusiasm the artisans even had a short-lived plan to rename New York "Hamiltoniana."

Surely this was a moment in which Alexander Hamilton must have felt that he had realized his boyhood dream of having "a place in the world." He was a true son of New York, the Constitution had been adopted, and the United States of America was now well on its way.

CHAPTER EIGHT

To Hamilton's great satisfaction, George Washington was elected president of the United States of America in February 1789. He began to appoint members to his cabinet. There would be three in all.

Washington asked Robert Morris, who had served previously as superintendent of finance, to be his secretary of the treasury. Morris declined, but said that he knew the perfect person for the job—someone close to Washington. When he said "Alexander Hamilton," Washington was surprised. "I always knew Colonel Hamilton to be a man of superior talents," Washington said, "but never supposed that he had

Washington, Hamilton, Knox, Jefferson

any knowledge of finance." Morris assured him that Hamilton was knowledgeable, so Washington asked thirty-four-year-old Alexander Hamilton to be his secretary of the treasury. He chose Thomas Jefferson as secretary of state and Henry Knox as secretary of war.

While Jefferson took his time before finally accepting, Hamilton jumped at the chance and accepted without hesitation. It was just the job he wanted. Taking care of the country's finances was a task that demanded organization and vision. Hamilton had both. It was not long before he had thirty-nine people working for him, while Jefferson had five and Knox only two.

Right away, Hamilton turned his attention to creating a customs service. In the early days of the republic, most of the revenue came from customs duties, or taxes, on goods coming in from other countries. The states raised most of their money this way. Now these taxes would be paid directly to the federal government, and Hamilton saw an immediate need for a department to collect them and make sure that there was no cheating. To prevent the smuggling of goods into the country, he outfitted lighthouses on the seacoast, had the buoys, beacons and piers at the ports put in good working order and had ten guard boats built to patrol the seas. This service was the forerunner of the Coast Guard.

Even though Hamilton and Jefferson served together as secretaries to Washington, their relationship had never been close and was not always easy. There had been several years of brisk controversy between them concerning all of Hamilton's financial proposals. They came from opposite positions on the role the federal government should play in the United States. Hamilton wanted a central government with strong leadership, while Jefferson favored a weaker federal government and strong states' rights.

This difference of opinion was never more obvious than on one night in June of 1790. After leaving President Washington's home, the two men found themselves outside together. Jefferson later described Hamilton as being uncharacteristically unkempt. He walked with Jefferson for upwards of an hour, pacing back and forth, talking about his anxiety for his assumption bill. Hamilton wanted Congress to agree to consolidate state and federal debts into one debt that the federal government would assume. But not all states thought this was fair, especially Virginia and the other southern states. Hamilton feared his assumption bill might not pass. If his plan was not approved, Hamilton felt he might have to resign.

The next day, Hamilton received an invitation to Jefferson's house for dinner. James Madison and several others were there and it became clear that they were willing to listen to some kind of proposal for a deal. Hamilton said that if Jefferson and Madison could get the assumption bill passed, he in turn would do his best to secure the nation's capital on the Potomac River in Virginia, which he knew would please the south. Hamilton had hoped for the capital to be in New York, but he would sacrifice that for the establishment of federal credit.

Madison at first demurred because Virginia had already paid most of its debts, but Hamilton explained that so had other states, and now they would all have to think about what was good for the United States. The deal went through and Washington, D.C., became the nation's capital. Philadelphia, and not New York, would be the temporary capital until the permanent one was built.

Hamilton was eager to have the country's public finances organized in a specific way. It was no surprise that he wanted to establish a central bank, which he called the Bank of the United States. After all, in 1784 he had already helped establish the Bank of New York. But there was much opposition to his proposal, especially among some of the Founding Fathers from agricultural states in the south, where Madison and Jefferson were from. Some people just didn't trust banks, calling them gambling centers. Hamilton himself was often accused of personally profiting from them, something he never did. One southerner remarked that he would just as soon be seen entering a house of ill repute as to be seen entering a bank. But Congress approved the bank bill and, despite Jefferson urging Washington to veto it, he signed the bill on February 14, 1791.

Hamilton had to come up with a way to raise money to fund the Bank of the United States. The bank would offer shares, or scrip, to investors, who would pay a modest fee and then pay the balance eighteen months later. On the day the scrip was to be issued, lines of people formed in front of the bank, all wishing to buy scrip. As successful as the offering was, there was still prejudice against banking, especially in the rural south. They didn't trust the business community in the north.

Hamilton also felt it was important for the United States to mint its own currency. At this time there was no U.S. monetary standard; all kinds of foreign money were in use. The U.S. dollar replaced the British pound and Hamilton created coins such as the dime, penny and half-penny. He

wanted to make sure that there were small denomination coins suitable for those with even the most modest means. He started the U.S. Mint in Philadelphia, where it stayed even after the capital was moved to Washington, D.C.

People who were quick to find fault with Hamilton must have been delighted when they found out he was not a perfect man. In the summer of 1791, a young woman named Maria Reynolds had gone to him for help. She needed money, she told him. Her husband was cruel to her, she said. And unfaithful. Hamilton not only gave her money, he went on seeing her. Eliza had left Philadelphia for Albany and Alexander must have been lonely without her. Then Maria's husband, James Reynolds, began blackmailing Hamilton over their relationship.

No one knew until a story came out in a newspaper six years later. Although Hamilton had stopped seeing Maria Reynolds long before, a reporter erroneously and vindictively wrote that Hamilton had been paying blackmail for cheating the government out of money. This was a stain on Hamilton's public reputation and honor, which he would not tolerate. Against the advice of friends, he published a ninety-five-page pamphlet with a detailed confession of the real reason for the blackmail, and included a copy of a personal letter to Maria Reynolds to prove it. He was willing to tell the whole story, revealing his private indiscretion, to save his public reputation and honor. However difficult this was for Eliza, eventually she must have accepted her husband's explanation, as hurtful as this must have been.

Hamilton saw American manufacturing as an important goal for the country. He watched industry grow like wildfire in England. He was convinced that to be a strong, independent nation, America needed to be able to supply its own manufactured goods. He remembered only too well how difficult it was to supply arms during the Revolution. But not everyone saw it this way. Jefferson and others wanted America to remain an agricultural nation. Hamilton saw the promise of both.

Hamilton looked over areas of the country that he thought were most suitable for manufacturing. He proposed New Jersey because its many waterfalls were a source of power, lots of people would be available to work in the mills and factories, and it was close to New York, a good place to raise money. He settled on the Great Falls of the Passaic River, a spot where he and Washington and Lafayette had stopped to rest and eat a picnic lunch in a quiet pause during the Revolution.

But Hamilton didn't just want to build mills and factories, he wanted to build a town. So a group chartered by the New Jersey legislature, the Society for Establishing Useful Manufacturers (SEUM), founded the city of Paterson, New Jersey, at the falls. Hamilton was the society's chief advisor and most active volunteer.

Unfortunately, Hamilton's plans for Paterson didn't succeed then, but in later years it became an important manufacturing center. In 1907 a statue of Alexander Hamilton was erected by the community to commemorate his contribution to the city's founding.

If only Hamilton had been recognized for this achievement during his lifetime. As it was, he found himself more and more the target of Jefferson and his emerging Republican Party, rebuffing claims of his being a "monarchist" whose financial policies reflected too much love for England, banking and manufacturing—all that they had fought against in the Revolution.

Then, in 1794 the country faced the possibility of insurrection from discontented farmers in western Pennsylvania. It would become known as the Whiskey Rebellion and was brought on by taxes suggested to the Congress by Hamilton.

Once the federal government had assumed the states' debts, Hamilton understood that he needed to raise more money. In late 1790, he suggested a tax on whiskey and other spirits. These taxes would be second only to custom duties in raising revenue. The following summer, the tax became a reality. The Pennsylvania farmers were furious. It wasn't fair, they said. They grew wheat and there was no way they could send it east over the mountains by wagonload, so they converted it to whiskey and sent it in kegs on the backs of donkeys and mules.

By 1792 the reaction to the whiskey tax started to get violent. Tax collectors found themselves being tarred and feathered and whipped. Once, angry farmers surrounded the house of a citizen who had rented his house to a tax collector and ordered him to get the man out, threatening terrible things if he didn't do what they said.

But the tax didn't go away. The farmers had had enough. They banded together and held a protest in Braddock's Field in Pittsburgh in 1794. They made it clear that they would not tolerate a whiskey tax. This was the kind of "mobocracy" that Hamilton had once been afraid of. Reluctantly, he felt it was time to use force. He appealed to President Washington for help.

At first, Washington thought he could send Secretary of War Henry Knox to the scene, but Knox pleaded that he had important business in Maine and couldn't do it. In the end, Washington decided that the militias of Virginia, Maryland and New Jersey should be called to quell the rebellion. It fell to Hamilton to stand in for Knox. With his usual skill, Hamilton single-handedly equipped the militias with everything from uniforms to blankets to muskets—and loved doing it.

Washington set out with Hamilton and went as far as Carlisle, Pennsylvania, before returning to Philadelphia at

the end of October, confident that the situation was in good hands. Hamilton continued on with Governor Henry Lee and an army of twelve thousand men. This show of force was enough. Governor Lee issued amnesty to all the ringleaders and Washington pardoned the rebellion's most influential leaders.

The Whiskey Rebellion had been stopped and Hamilton felt that the country was back on the track of stability. Soon after, in December, he resigned from his position as secretary of the treasury and indicated that he was through with public life. Eliza wasn't well, he needed to earn more money and he wanted to spend more time with his family. During his five years as the first secretary of the treasury, he had accomplished much for his adopted country: the establishment of the Bank of the United States and the U.S. Mint, the formation of a Coast Guard and Customs Service, as well as the passing of the assumption bill to successfully deal with the country's debt. Hamilton had been instrumental in laying the foundation for a new American government and served as a wise counsel to President Washington.

Eliza's sister, Angelica, wrote to her from England, wondering why Alexander was stepping down. She suspected that Eliza had advised him to do so and she half scolded her. She suggested that when she returned to America, she and

Eliza would have to compensate Alexander by making sure he had fun. They would not talk politics, she said, "a little agreeable nonsense will do us more good."

But Angelica should have realized that Alexander could not completely leave public life. He continued to write essays for the newspaper, and at the end of March 1796, Washington asked him to draft his farewell address to the country. He would not run for a third term. At the end of his first administration, when Washington thought he would not run again, he had asked Madison to draft such an address. But he had run for a second term after all. Washington may have hurt Madison by asking Hamilton this time. In any case, Hamilton did draft it, but he asked Washington to look at Madison's as well and decide which address he wanted to use. There was no question that Washington wanted Hamilton's version; however, Washington had to cut down Hamilton's text, saying it was too long. Washington didn't intend to deliver the address, but to have it appear in newspapers throughout the country. Years later, when both Washington and Hamilton had passed away, Eliza proudly revealed her husband's hand in writing this famous text.

Among other things, the address emphasized the need for the new country of America to remain neutral in international conflicts. John Jay returned from England with a treaty he had negotiated with the British, who had been seizing American ships in the Caribbean. The treaty was unpopular everywhere. Many people claimed that Jay had not been fair to America. He had given away too much. Jay remarked that anyone could find their way across the country by the light of his burning effigies. In New York, a discussion in the street about the treaty developed into a stone-throwing mob scene. Hamilton was there, and instead of calming things down, which normally would have been his natural response, he only made it worse by challenging to fight them all, one by one.

Not long after the Jay Treaty was formally signed, America had to turn its attention to France. England had been the first to capture American ships in the Caribbean, and in 1797 France followed suit.

Jefferson and his Republicans were supportive of the French and the French Revolution, despite its bloody aftermath. The Federalists, including Hamilton, were concerned that France was posturing for war. By the spring of 1797, the French had seized over three hundred American vessels and had expelled the new American minister to France. John Adams, now president, delivered a highly derogatory speech to Congress denouncing these actions.

In August, he sent a delegation of three men to France:

two Federalists, Thomas Pinckney and John Marshall, and one Republican, Eldridge Gerry. The delegation was met, then ignored. After a while, the French sent three underlings (known in America by the code names X, Y and Z) to the American delegation with these demands:

1. President Adams should retract the controversial passages of his speech.

2. America should extend a large loan to France.

3. America should pay for the damages to American ships caused by French privateers.

In response, Adams reluctantly authorized the formation of an American army. Adams wanted George Washington in charge, and Washington would agree only if Alexander Hamilton was second in command. Adams didn't like Hamilton, but he needed Washington, so he agreed. Washington made Hamilton inspector general with the rank of major general. The warm relationship between the two had been reestablished in the years following the Revolution, and Washington had resumed his habit of asking Hamilton's advice.

John Adams, who had never been a military man, began appearing in uniform. Adams was preparing for war but very much wanted peace. Eldridge Gerry, who had stayed in France when the other delegates returned to America, apparently convinced the French government that America really wanted peace, so the French backed down.

Hamilton, of course, had not been sorry that there had been preparations for war and that he was in the thick of those preparations. When the threat was lifted, he put aside his military uniform one more time and settled once again into American politics.

Endings

CHAPTER NINE

The election of 1800 was famous for being close. Thomas Jefferson and Aaron Burr, Republicans, were both running for president, as were Federalists John Adams and Thomas Pinckney. Hamilton did not want Adams for a second term and even went so far as to work against his reelection. Even though Adams was a Federalist, Hamilton strongly disagreed with many of Adams's policies. And certainly Adams had no love for Hamilton.

Adams lost to Jefferson by eight electoral votes. But Jefferson and Burr each received seventy-three votes, so it was up to the House of Representatives to break the tie. Early on Hamilton decided that he would vote for Jefferson, even though he had crossed political swords with him so often. Despite their differences, Hamilton felt that Jefferson would not make a dangerous president but Burr would. For a long time Hamilton had distrusted Burr. While secretary of the treasury, Hamilton had once complained of being short of money and Burr had impatiently reminded him that in his public capacity, money passed over his desk all the time—how easy to just help himself. Ever mindful of the honor entrusted to him, this had been an early indication to Hamilton that Burr was not trustworthy.

It took twenty-six ballots in the House of Representatives before the election results were finally determined. Jefferson became the new president and Burr the vice president. Even Jefferson had little confidence in his own vice president and Burr found himself sidelined and not included in political decisions.

Soon, however, something happened that erased the country's problems from Hamilton's mind. His oldest—and favorite—son Philip was in trouble. At a Fourth of July celebration in 1801, a Jefferson supporter, George Eacker, made a speech in which he claimed that Hamilton's army had been formed to frighten American citizens about a trumped-up foreign invasion. Philip took exception to the references to his father and in November he confronted Eacker while he was watching a theatrical performance in New York.

Subsequently, the two men agreed to settle their differences with a duel. Hamilton must have been disturbed when he found out. He was strongly against dueling, although he had been involved in duels six times, either in the negotiations or as a second. Still, he believed vehemently in upholding one's honor and came out of a military background where dueling was an accepted way of life. Only a coward would refuse a duel.

But here was his nineteen-year-old son dueling to protect his father's reputation. Hamilton knew that not all duels ended in death. Often they were a means of solving a confrontation without either person losing face. He told Philip to waste his shot in the hopes of ending the matter with honor and without bloodshed.

Philip borrowed a pair of dueling pistols from his uncle, John Church, Angelica's husband. The two men with their seconds met on a sandbar near present-day Jersey City. Philip held his fire, but Eacker didn't. Philip was mortally wounded. When Hamilton learned of the outcome, he rushed to his doctor's house seeking medical assistance for Philip, only to faint in the doctor's office. Philip died the next day. Alexander was devastated; Eliza was inconsolable. She was expecting her eighth child in six months (she would name him Philip). At the funeral, Alexander had to be supported on both sides.

In the months following, Hamilton had trouble settling down to his busy schedule. He was a prominent, successful New York lawyer and had clients who needed him. Even after he left public service, Hamilton couldn't sever his political ties. Now he began to write and publish a series of articles analyzing and criticizing Jefferson's policies. He had done the same thing with John Adams after his term in office had expired.

Once again, Hamilton tried to find more time to spend with his family. He purchased fifteen acres of land in upper Manhattan, nine miles north of his office. Here he built a home for his family, completed in 1802, and called it the Grange, after his grandparents' home in Scotland, as well as his uncle James Lytton's plantation in St. Croix.

"A disappointed politician is very apt to take refuge in a garden," Alexander told a friend, and he began learning about plants and landscaping from his friend Dr. Hosack, who had recently established a botanical garden. Known for his frugality, Alexander spent more lavishly on the Grange than he ever had. And he spent more and more time with his family.

In 1803, President Jefferson negotiated with France for the purchase of a huge tract of western lands known as the Louisiana Purchase, which doubled the size of the country. New Englanders soon became concerned that slavery would be extended into the new territories and there was talk of a northern secession. Hamilton saw this as a threat to the Union and viewed the secessionist movement "with horror."

In 1804 there was an election coming up about which Hamilton also felt strongly. Aaron Burr again! Now he was running for governor of New York. If he won, Hamilton wondered, might he not try again later to run for president?

In March, Hamilton dined with Judge Taylor in Albany. Also present were James Kent and Dr. Charles Cooper. Cooper was much interested in hearing Kent and Hamilton talk so frankly of their opinions of Burr. Subsequently, Cooper reported this conversation in a letter to a friend of his and this letter was published in a newspaper.

Aaron Burr read the letter and took exception to Cooper's

report that Hamilton had called him "despicable." Burr wrote to Hamilton, asking for an explanation. His letter had the tone of a prelude to a duel, but Hamilton treated it as only an interruption in his busy schedule.

In the end, Burr asked Hamilton to list all the derogatory statements that he had made against him over the years. Since the two men had been political rivals for more than fifteen years, this was not only impossible but an unreasonable request and Hamilton simply ended the correspondence.

Shortly, however, Hamilton received a final letter from Burr that included a challenge to a duel. Hamilton might have replied that he was opposed to dueling, but at the same time he did not want to give anyone a chance to call him a coward. So he accepted. Just as he had advised his son Philip, he told Nathaniel Pendleton and his friend Rufus King that he would not fire at Burr. As much as they tried to talk him out of it, Hamilton refused.

The two men selected their seconds and set the date for July 11 in a secluded dueling ground at Weehawken, New Jersey, a place often used for these confrontations. Dueling was against the law in both New York and New Jersey, but was treated more seriously in New York. So although they had taken care to choose New Jersey, they were careful in every way to hide the nature of what was going on.

Just a week before the duel, a meeting of the Society of Cincinnati, made up of retired army officers, was held in New York. After Washington died in 1799, Hamilton had been made the president of the society and never missed these meetings. He put on his dress uniform and his plumed helmet and was ready for all the nostalgic talk that such occasions always elicited.

Toward the end of the evening, Hamilton's old army friends pushed him toward the large table in the center of the room. Hamilton knew what was expected of him. He jumped on top of the table and led everyone as they sang what was now known as the "Valley Forge Song." "How stands the glass around?" they sang. It would have been hard to believe that Hamilton was planning to go to the dueling grounds in Weehawken within the week. Aaron Burr was at the meeting too, but he sat stone faced and silent through most of it.

On July 4 Alexander wrote a letter to Eliza:

This letter, my very dear Eliza, will not be delivered to you unless I shall first have terminated my earthly career; to begin, as I humbly hope from redeeming grace and divine mercy, a happy immortality.

If it had been possible for me to have avoided

*the interview, my love for you and my precious
children would have been alone a decisive motive.
But it was not possible, without sacrifices, which
would have rendered me unworthy of your esteem. I
need not tell you of the pangs I feel, from the idea of
quitting you and exposing you to the anguish which
I know you would feel. Nor could I dwell on the
topic lest it should unman me.*

*The consolations of Religion, my beloved, can
alone support you; and these you have a right
to enjoy. Fly to the bosom of your God and be
comforted. With my last idea, I shall cherish the
sweet hope of meeting you in a better world.*

*Adieu best of wives and best of Women. Embrace
all my darling Children for me.*

Ever yours, AH

In the days leading up to the duel, Alexander spent many quiet hours at home in the company of his family at the Grange, cherishing the comfort that his wife and children brought to him.

The night before the duel Alexander returned to their house on Wall Street. Before going to bed, he sat down at his desk to write another letter to Eliza. He left instructions that this letter also was not to be read until after the duel. He wrote:

> *The Scruples of a Christian have determined me*
> *to expose my own life to any extent rather than subject*
> *myself to the guilt of taking the life of another. This*
> *must increase my hazards & redoubles my pangs for*
> *you. But you had rather I should die innocent than*
> *live guilty. Heaven can preserve me and I humbly*
> *hope will, but in the contrary event, I charge you to*
> *remember that you are a Christian. God's will be*
> *done! The will of a merciful God must be good.*
> *Once more Adieu My Darling darling Wife,*
> *AH*

The next morning, Hamilton rose before daylight. He called for his servant to help him put on his dress uniform and boots. He picked up John Church's pistols (the same pistols that his son Philip had used) and ordered his carriage to be brought to the door.

Hamilton was met by his second, Nathaniel Pendleton, and his physician, Dr. Hosack. Together they rode the short distance to the waterfront where his boat was waiting. The four oarsmen pushed off across the water that still held the quiet of the leftover night. There was little conversation in the boat, but Hamilton could only have been filled with thoughts of the destiny that was ahead of him. This was not the end that he had planned for himself, he may have thought. Or was it? John Laurens would have known the answer.

Aaron Burr, with his second, William Van Ness, went to Weehawken in a separate boat. They arrived on the small shore at the foot of the Palisades a half hour before Hamilton and climbed up to the narrow ledge hidden by trees. They used their boots to scrape away the leaves and dead branches. Then Hamilton and Pendleton arrived and climbed up, leaving Dr. Hosack at the boat.

Hamilton and Burr took their places ten paces apart. They stood in profile to each other, the position most used in a duel because it made the person harder to hit. As the challenged party, Hamilton had his choice of place. He had chosen the north side of the dueling grounds, a poor decision as the sun was in his eyes, giving the advantage to Burr, who had the sun behind him.

Hamilton called for a pause. "Stop. In certain states of light one requires glasses." From his pocket he pulled out his glasses, made a small show of practicing his aim, then said he was ready. The call was made: "Present!"

Two shots rang through the air simultaneously (or so it seemed). Burr's arrived first. It went to its mark, hitting Hamilton above his right hip. He fell to the ground. Hamilton's bullet, which he didn't remember firing and may have gone off when he fell, sailed above Burr's head and buried itself in a tree branch.

Dr. Hosack, upon hearing the shots, rushed up to the ledge. He went immediately to Hamilton's side. "It is a mortal wound, doctor," Hamilton whispered and then lost consciousness as he was carried down to the boat.

As they crossed the river Dr. Hosack gave Hamilton

some smelling salts, and as the breeze picked up, Hamilton regained consciousness, complaining that his vision was poor and his legs didn't work.

They were going to the home of Hamilton's friend William Bayard, who lived in a house close to the river and who had seen the men cross the river earlier that morning. James Bayard, his face streaming with tears, met them at the front door, directing them to a bedroom where a bed had been made ready. Hamilton, rousing himself, asked that Mrs. Hamilton be called. "But don't alarm her," he said.

Hamilton was in great pain and when he complained of his back, the doctor removed his clothes and discovered that the bullet had traveled through his rib then to his liver, finally settling in his spine. He was given laudanum for his pain and weak wine for strength.

A despairing Eliza sat by Alexander's bedside through the night and into the next day. When she realized that the end was near, she called in the children. Eliza held little Philip while the other children arranged themselves at the foot of his bed: Angelica, Alexander, John, James, William and Elizabeth. Alexander looked at these beloved children, then, as if he could not bear the sight, he closed his eyes. In a short while, Alexander Hamilton was gone.

It was the largest funeral that had ever been held in New

York up until that time. Ships in the harbor lowered their flags to half-mast, firing guns echoed from the Battery, church bells tolled, and the Bank of New York was draped in black. Two New York militia units and various clergymen, followed by the Society of Cincinnati, led the funeral procession. Two little black boys in white turbans walked in front of the casket, which, in turn, was followed by Hamilton's gray horse, his master's boots and spurs reversed in the  stirrups. Then came his older sons and, behind them, New Yorkers from all walks of life. It was two hours before they reached Trinity Church.

Two chairs stood side by side on the stage of Trinity Church—one for Hamilton's brother-in-law, John Church, and one for Gouverneur Morris, his good friend. Morris had been asked to give the address. He drew a detailed and loving picture of Hamilton, citing his many unique qualities and contributions, but also acknowledging his failings, which may have led many in the audience to nod their heads and perhaps sometimes smile in forgiveness. Of course, he also spoke of Hamilton's steadfast love for his country and his loyalty to New York. He spoke to a tearful crowd who seemed to recognize what an extraordinary man Hamilton had been.

Forty-nine-year-old Alexander Hamilton died at two in the afternoon on Thursday, July 12, 1804. On his deathbed, among his last words, he spoke of his beloved America, "If they break this Union, they will break my heart." How could anyone have thought that Alexander Hamilton was an outsider?

Notes

p. 12 There is some uncertainty with regard to the year of Hamilton's birth. Although some evidence exists that he was born in 1755, Hamilton himself always claimed that he was born in 1757. Perhaps when he went to college in America, he chose to not appear older than his classmates.

p. 22 The Sons of Liberty, also known as the Liberty Boys, was a secret organization of American patriots who resisted British taxes and laws, frequently through large public demonstrations. They were widely accused of tarring and feathering their opponents.

p. 22 King's College was founded in New York, New York, in 1754 by royal charter of King George II of England. The American Revolution forced suspension of instruction in 1776; it was reopened in 1784 with a new name: Columbia University.

p. 23 The College of New Jersey was founded in Elizabeth, New Jersey, in 1746 by royal charter of King George II of England. The college moved to Princeton, New Jersey, in 1756 and changed its name to Princeton University in 1896.

p. 24 Young Aaron Burr suffered multiple family losses. Soon after smallpox struck his father and grandfather, his mother also died of smallpox, and within months his grandmother died of dysentery. His uncle, Timothy Edwards, raised Burr, who was orphaned at two years old.

p. 25 British taxation was just as important to New Yorkers as it was to Bostonians. Rebels from extralegal committees in the City of New York held their own tea party when the merchant ship *Nancy* arrived off Sandy Hook in April 1884, several months after the more well-known event in Boston. Alexander McDougall, under whom Hamilton would later serve, played a central role in the taking of the vessel.

p. 26   Tories were also called Loyalists.

p. 30   The Battle of Bunker Hill actually took place primarily on neighboring Breed's Hill. Although it seems that Bunker Hill was the original objective, the Americans, apparently by mistake, stealthily fortified Breed's Hill, located southeast of Bunker Hill, and this is where most of the battle took place. Although typically referred to as the Battle of Bunker Hill, it is also known as the Battle of Breed's Hill.

p. 39   Hamilton felt strongly about proper military dress. Later in life he wrote, "Nothing is more necessary than to stimulate the vanity of soldiers. To this end a smart dress is essential. When not attended to, the soldier is exposed to ridicule and humiliation."

p. 40   England, lacking sufficient numbers of soldiers to fight in America, contracted with several German states to enlist soldiers. The majority of the seventeen thousand German mercenaries were from Hesse-Cassell and were known as Hessians.

p. 63   Hamilton soon became indispensable to Washington as his aide. Washington had previously written to Congress "that I am obliged to neglect many other essential parts of my duty. It is absolutely necessary . . . for me to have persons that can think for me, as well as execute orders." He found that in Hamilton.

p. 69   The Marquis de Lafayette was a young French nobleman who believed so fervently in the cause of freedom that he joined the Continental army under General Washington in the spring of 1777. Lafayette, Laurens and Hamilton were fast friends.

p. 70   A poltroon is a coward.

p. 76   Hamilton and Laurens both felt strongly that the emancipation of slaves was tied into the larger struggle for freedom, as well as acknowledging slaves as a source of military manpower. Laurens was the son of a slaveholder and Hamilton had been exposed to slavery as a boy in the West Indies.

p. 80   Peggy Arnold was allowed to return to her home in Philadelphia. Benedict Arnold, whose name has since become synonymous with the word *traitor*, joined the British army and fought against the Americans. After the war, he and his wife sailed to London. The Arnolds spent their remaining years back and forth between England and Canada. Arnold died in 1801.

p. 99   It was common during this time period for people to publish anonymously or to use pseudonyms.

p. 130 Eliza Hamilton lived to be ninety-seven. She was buried next to Alexander in the Trinity churchyard in New York.

Historical Reproduction Credits

The American Revolution: A Picture Sourcebook by John Grafton, courtesy of Dover Publications, Inc., New York, 1975: pp. 27, 34–35, 41, 46–47, 53, 57, 60–61, 66, 67, 70, 78, 79, 81, 86, 100. ✳ Courtesy of Columbia University Archives: p. 22 *The first campus of King's College at Trinity Church in Lower Manhattan* by E. P. Chrystie. ✳ Library of Congress: p. 13 A. Hamilton, drawn from life, Jan. 11, 1773; p. 122 Hamilton Grange, (Moved From) 237 West 141 Street to 141st Street & Amsterdam, New York, NY; p. 131 Trinity Church. ✳ Courtesy of the National Guard Bureau, Historical Services Division, Arlington, Virginia: p. 110 *...To Execute the Laws of the Union ... (The Whiskey Rebellion),* painted by Donna Neary. ✳ National Oceanic and Atmospheric Administration/Department of Commerce: p. 18 *Ouragon.* ✳ New York Public Library: pp. 116–117 *View of New York from Weehawken,* circa 1828, by R. Wallis. ✳ Courtesy of Ian Schoenherr: p. 29 *Hamilton Addressing the Mob* by Howard Pyle, from *Harper's New Monthly Magazine,* October 1884; p. 32 *In 1776—The Conflagration* by Howard Pyle, from *Harper's New Monthly Magazine,* June 1893; p. 95 Aaron Burr portrait, artist unknown, from *Harper's Encyclopedia of United States History,* Harper & Brothers, 1902; p. 102 Illustration of Washington's Cabinet by Howard Pyle, from *Harper's New Monthly Magazine,* November 1896; p. 129 *Duel Between Hamilton and Burr,* artist unknown, from *Building the Nation* by Charles Carleton Coffin, Harper & Brothers, 1883; p. 132 *Where Hamilton Fell,* artist unknown, from *Building the Nation* by Charles Carleton Coffin, Harper & Brothers, 1883. ✳ United States National Archives: p. 38 *Provincial Company, New York, Artillery, Captain Alexander Hamilton, 1776,* by D. Falls; p. 54 Surrender of the Hessian Troops to General Washington, after The Battle of Trenton, December 1776; p. 65 Hamilton, Mrs. Alexander (seated pose), 1781. ✳ wikipedia.com: p. 8–9 *A Map of the West Indies,* 1736, by Herman Moll. ✳ © Archiving Early America, http://earlyamerica.com: p. 42 *The Thirteen Colonies in 1775.*

Bibliography

Brookhiser, Richard. *Alexander Hamilton, American*. New York, Sydney, London: Simon & Schuster, 1999.

Chernow, Ron. *Alexander Hamilton*. New York: Penguin Books, 2004.

Ellis, Joseph J. *Founding Brothers: The Revolutionary Generation*. New York: Random House, 2000.

Flexner, James Thomas. *The Young Hamilton*. Boston & Toronto: Little Brown & Co., 1978.

Kennedy, Roger C. *Burr, Hamilton & Jefferson: A Study in Character*. Oxford: Oxford University Press, 2000.

Kline, Mary-Jo, ed. *Alexander Hamilton, A Biography in His Own Words*. New York: Newsweek, Inc., 1973.

McCullough, David. *1776*. New York, London, Toronto, Sydney: Simon & Schuster, 2005.

Morris, Richard B., ed. *Alexander Hamilton and the Founding of a Nation*. New York: The Dial Press, 1957.

Index